£5.99
UK only

Edited by Jane Clempner
Designed by Sheryl Bone

© 2001 Bluenet Limited
Published in Great Britain in 2001
by Egmont Books Limited,
239 Kensington High Street,
London, W8 6SA

Printed in Italy
ISBN 0 7498 53433

westlife™
The Annual 2002

CONTENTS

westlife ™

Just three years ago, Westlife were five boys from Ireland with big ideas. Now they are international stars, record breakers and multi award winners! Their worldwide success is a result of pure talent. The year 2000 saw Westlife clocking up their seventh consecutive number one single and celebrating a number one album. In 2001 Westlife released another successful album and took to the road proving their worth as live performers. Clearly, there is no stopping the pop phenomenon called Westlife...

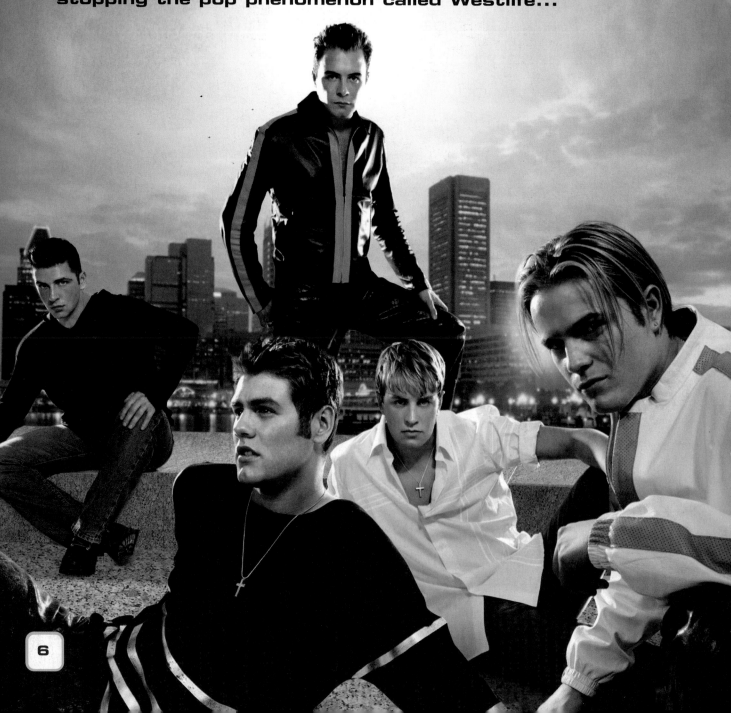

Bryan

Mark

Kian

Nicky

7

 # Luck of the Irish

With three successful albums under their belt and eight consecutive single releases reaching the number one slot, Westlife have achieved more in three years than most might hope to achieve in a lifetime. So how does this kind of success happen and where did it all start?

The story of Westlife begins in the town of Sligo in West Ireland, two hours from Dublin. Best known as the birth place of poet William Yeats, it was in Sligo that Shane Filan, Kian Egan and Mark Feehily grew up. In their early years, they appeared on stage together in a local theatre's production of Grease. "During the interval we would come on and do pop covers," says Shane. It was at the after show party the idea was born of singing together in a band. The result was Six as One. Three other guys joined – Derek, Graham and Michael – and together they played their first gig at the Southern Hotel, Sligo.

Local heroes

Their popularity grew and now, under the name of IO YOU, the boys wrote and recorded the song 'Together Girl Forever'. Sales in their home town were encouraging, and the band were approached by two managers looking for new talent. But Shane was concerned with the terms. He was wise in holding back. His mum had been sending copies of 'Together Girl Forever' to Boyzone's manager, Louis Walsh, and her persistence paid off! In 1998, Louis agreed to see the band.

Clearly impressed, Louis offered the boys the support slot on the Boyzone tour at Christmas. They were ecstatic! First however, they were to support Backstreet Boys in Dublin in March. The boys performed three songs – 'Together Girl Forever', 'Everlasting Love' and 'Pinball Wizard'. The show proved a turning point in their careers as they got their first taste of fame. After initially announcing he wouldn't be taking on another boy band after Boyzone, Louis agreed to manage IO YOU. However, he wanted a five piece group and so, to Derek's disappointment, he was dropped from the band.

From here on, the group's development was rapid. With Louis as manager, they worked hard recording songs for demo tapes to play to record companies. It was around this time Ronan Keating became involved. He had heard about Louis' latest signing and wanted to meet the band and help choose their recording material. To the boys' delight, Ronan asked to help manage the young band he got on so well with.

New recruits

Under new management, the band needed some fine tuning and it was decided to let another of the original boys go. This time it was Graham. Kian remembers when he heard the decision. "I felt terrible," he says. "He was my best friend. I couldn't tell him myself, so Louis had to do it."

With a space to fill, auditions were held in Dublin for a fifth member. On Saturday 19th June, around 300 people arrived at the Red Box. Amongst them were two hopefuls – Nicky Byrne and Bryan McFadden. Dressed in a smart black suit, Nicky chose to sing 'Father and Son' and, despite coming in too early, he pulled off the rest of the song. Bryan also impressed everyone and consequently the choice was difficult. "I remember saying to Nicky at the audition, 'May the best man win'. We were both so keen to be part of the band," says Bryan. According to Shane: "There was no contest. We knew we had found the missing pieces." And so it was that Nicky and Bryan were invited to join the boys and see how they hit it off. IO YOU returned to Sligo a six piece band.

Disappointment was to follow for Michael. Now that two new members had joined, he was the next to go. Understandably, he was devastated and it took a long time for him to come to terms with the rejection.

It's a deal

With the line up finally complete and a new name Westside, swiftly changed to Westlife because of a copyright issue in the US, the boys secured the record deal they wanted. They had already met with Simon Cowell of RCA on previous rounds of meetings as IO YOU. However at that stage, he was not happy with the look of the band. This time, not surprisingly, he was ready to sign.

The tour with Boyzone firmly established Westlife on the pop ladder. In fact it was said the new group was stealing the show! They performed 'Swear It Again', 'Flying Without Wings', 'Everybody Knows' and 'If I Let You Go'. Media interest grew rapidly, as well as a huge female fan following. A tour of under-18s clubs followed, then a BBC roadshow and the Smash Hits Roadshow where they won the award for Best New Tour Act.

The boys started recording their first album in the early part of 1999. Their first single 'Swear It Again' was initially released in Ireland, where it achieved number one status, and then in the UK where the success was repeated. Kian looks back: "It really was a tremendous time for us. Winning the Smash Hits award was a great start and then to achieve a number one with our first single was amazing." Clearly, Westlife were here to stay.

9

PASSPORT

shane

Full name:	Shane Steven Filan
Date of birth:	5th July 1979
Star sign:	Cancer
Place of birth:	Sligo, Ireland
Height:	5ft 9in
Colour of eyes:	Hazel
Parents:	Mae and Peter
Siblings:	3 brothers - Finbarr, Peter, Liam 3 sisters - Yvonne, Denise, Mairead
Pets:	2 German Shepherds, Kaiser and Oscar; horses
Education:	Scoil Fatima, St John's, Summerhill College, Limerick Regional College
Previous job(s):	Working in the family restaurant, hardware store assistant
First record bought:	Billy Joel's 'Uptown Girl'
Likes:	Christmas, shopping, watching 'Friends' on TV
Dislikes:	Rude people, coffee
Worst habit:	Daydreaming
Sports:	Horseriding, football
Car:	BMW
Favourite place in the world:	Sligo

KIAN:
UP CLOSE AND PERSONAL

*"I don't feel like a celebrity...
I just happen to be in a famous band."*

It's no surprise Kian found himself in a musical career. He comes from a large, musically talented family and was encouraged from a very early age.

As a child, Kian learnt to play the saxophone, flute, clarinet, guitar and bass. He is particularly good at the piano (he reached grade eight) and was taught by his brother, Gavin, who is a professional teacher. Marielle, Kian's younger sister, is following in her brother's footsteps by learning piano and violin. Kian's closest brother, Tom, also plays in a rock band. As music was always being played at home it naturally became part of Kian's life.
His mum, Patricia, says he was a determined child and succeeded at most things he did, whether it was singing, acting or dancing.

Finding drama

By the age of four, Kian was on stage reciting poetry.
In the years that followed, he took speech and drama classes.
Growing up in Sligo, Kian was really close to his cousins, in
particular Gillian who lived just around the corner. With Gillian,
Kian started getting into variety shows and musicals. "We used
to mess around in these community halls teaching kids how to
dance," Kian remembers.

In his younger days, Kian liked to be in charge. He was always
leader of the pack with his cousins and friends and ready for
an adventure, hence the scar under his right eye. The cause?
Hurtling down a hill at top speed on the bar of a bike and
smashing into a wall! Kian also found drama at the swimming
pool. Here he nearly drowned after being pushed in at the deep
end... luckily his sister was on hand to come to the rescue!

The Egan family say Kian was always singing around the house
and generally being noisy. Many a time his parents had to tell
him to turn down the music, especially when he got into
heavy metal!

Showstopper

Kian admits he was a bit of a terror at school and was often in trouble. The part of his education he enjoyed most was performing in plays! At primary school he usually managed to secure the lead. As his confidence grew, he took the lead in secondary school shows too. In total, he performed in ten shows, each time winning a more important role. In one of many productions of Grease, Kian played Kenickie, Shane took the lead as Danny and Mark played Vince Fontaine. Kian says acting played a huge part in his life and is certainly something he'd like to go back to.

Kian managed to put his mischievous and cheeky nature to work later in life when he took a job as a Kissagram! It was at the suggestion of a friend who performed with Kian and so he gave it a try. Kian recalls wearing a pair of see-through trousers with checked boxers and a little dickie bow. "It was actually a really good laugh," he says, "and I suppose it prepared me for the screaming girls of the future!"

Taking control

When the original band were looking for a fifth member, Kian worked with Louis, their manager, to find the right person. He certainly enjoyed being in control and put Nicky and Bryan through their paces. "I fired all these questions at the lads," he remembers. "I thought I was so cool!"

Now he says the boys in Westlife are like brothers – they argue, fight and muck around all the time. Kian says they've all had to grow up pretty fast to deal with the business that comes with being in a pop band – the lawyers, accountants and the media. Kian has been named the most business-like in the band and he takes fame in his stride. He says Westlife have matured as a group and are individually exercising their own ideas.

Despite going on the odd shopping spree, for which he is famous, Kian wisely invests the money he has earned with Westlife. He says being with the band has obviously changed his life dramatically, but performing in front of thousands of fans has always been his goal ever since he was a little kid.

Nowadays, the Egan house is a regular spot for fans to hang out and Kian's mum, Patricia, says there's always plenty of mail waiting for Kian when he comes home. His bedroom is full of teddies and presents fans have sent. Kian's parents are extremely proud of their son and what he has achieved. In response, Kian can rave on for hours about the respect he has for his mum and dad. He says he owes them a lot, particularly his mum who was the one who really got him into performing.

PASSPORT

Nicky

Full name:	Nicholas Bernard James Adam Byrne
Date of birth:	9th October 1978
Star sign:	Libra
Place of birth:	Dublin, Ireland
Height:	5ft 10in
Colour of eyes:	Blue
Distinguishing feature(s):	Scar on right elbow
Parents:	Yvonne and Nikki
Siblings:	1 brother - Adam 1 sister - Gillian
Education:	Baldoyle Bous National School, St Neasain's, St Plunkett's College
Previous job(s):	Goalkeeper with Leeds United, karaoke compere
First record bought:	Kylie Minogue's 'I Should Be So Lucky'
Likes:	Shopping, Japanese food, Elizabeth Hurley
Dislikes:	Ignorant people, smoking, heights
Worst habit:	Being forgetful, getting bored easily
Sports:	Football, golf, snooker, fishing
Car:	Blue Mercedes
Favourite place in the world:	Dublin

Music in the making

When Ronan Keating heard the Westlife sound, he asserted his belief in the band by taking a management role. "Nothing prepared me for how good they were, I knew I had to be involved," he said.

Ronan is now concentrating on his solo career and has taken a step back from Westlife. As Nicky says, "We've come so far and gained so much experience, we're now finding our feet, just as Ronan did for himself." In fact, what Westlife achieved in just a year, namely six number ones, it took Boyzone six years to achieve. That is not to undermine the value of Ronan's presence. He gave the boys sound advice and confidence through their early careers. He said at the time, "Westlife are set to be the next big Irish act on the international scene." Confidence indeed.

Masters of pop

From their first album recording, Westlife have worked with some of the most established names in pop. International producers Max Martin, Pete Waterman, Steve Mac and Wayne Hector worked with the boys on their debut album. Pete Waterman, who worked with '80s popstars Kylie Minogue, Rick Astley and Jason Donovan and more recently Steps, remembers first hearing Westlife. "When I heard 'Swear It Again', I was really excited," he says. "Here were five very unique and different voices."

Steve Mac, producer and songwriter, was also full of praise. "The boys were a dream to work with, they could sing anything we threw at them. We wrote 'Flying Without Wings' in just three hours." Mark remembers the debut recording: "It was a great learning experience for us and the producers gave us the inspiration to produce our own material in the future."

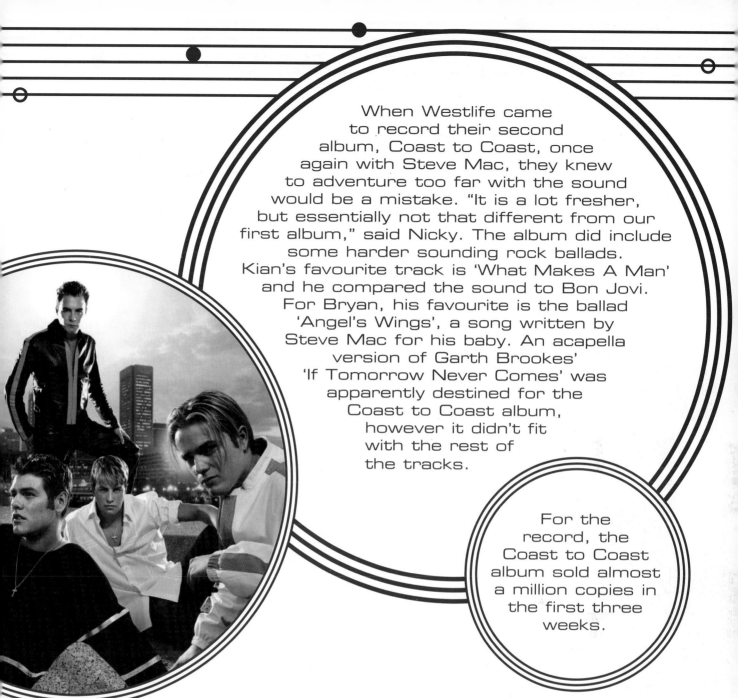

When Westlife came to record their second album, Coast to Coast, once again with Steve Mac, they knew to adventure too far with the sound would be a mistake. "It is a lot fresher, but essentially not that different from our first album," said Nicky. The album did include some harder sounding rock ballads. Kian's favourite track is 'What Makes A Man' and he compared the sound to Bon Jovi. For Bryan, his favourite is the ballad 'Angel's Wings', a song written by Steve Mac for his baby. An acapella version of Garth Brookes' 'If Tomorrow Never Comes' was apparently destined for the Coast to Coast album, however it didn't fit with the rest of the tracks.

For the record, the Coast to Coast album sold almost a million copies in the first three weeks.

Listening and learning

Kian recognises that his family were a great influence on him musically. "There was always music playing at home," he says. Kian's brother is actually a professional piano teacher and taught Kian to grade eight. Kian also has grade three in guitar. However, he says he's not a classical man, his love is playing rock guitar. Patricia Egan encouraged her sons to take as many music lessons as possible, so young Kian learnt saxophone, flute and clarinet, as well as guitar and bass. At the age of about 14, like the rest of the Westlife boys, Kian was into sounds such as Backstreet Boys and Take That. "We used to do lots of shows with covers of bands like Boyzone and Take That and then a few of our own songs," he says. By the age of 17, Kian was getting into the heavier sounds of Bon Jovi, Metallica and Guns 'N Roses.

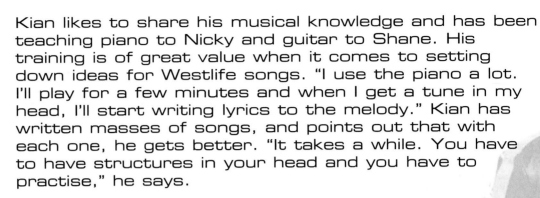

Kian likes to share his musical knowledge and has been teaching piano to Nicky and guitar to Shane. His training is of great value when it comes to setting down ideas for Westlife songs. "I use the piano a lot. I'll play for a few minutes and when I get a tune in my head, I'll start writing lyrics to the melody." Kian has written masses of songs, and points out that with each one, he gets better. "It takes a while. You have to have structures in your head and you have to practise," he says.

As for Nicky, showbiz has always been part of his life. His dad was in a band called Nikki and the Studs and young Nicky was often seen setting up the gear and watching in the wings. Nicky's musical influences come from the '80s. He says his favourites were Jason Donovan and Kylie Minogue! In fact, the first record he ever bought was Kylie's 'I Should Be So Lucky'. Nicky also spent a lot of time listening to his sister's faves, Bros and Aha. "I used to dance around my room pretending I was on stage in East 17!" he admits. Top of Nicky's current playlist are Backstreet Boys, The Cranberries and The Corrs.

Shane grew up to the sounds of Jim Reeves and Joseph Locke, his dad's favourites. He followed in his dad's footsteps, he was always singing around the house and occasionally on stage in showbands. Apparently Shane made himself a little microphone at the age of four and would sing to his heart's content in the family home, first Billy Joel numbers and then songs by his hero, Michael Jackson. Shane's mum, Mae, remembers a time when she would send Shane off upstairs to do his homework only to find him minutes later writing songs.

Mark's dad was an avid record collector and so from an early age Mark was surrounded by music. "My dad had all kinds of stuff, from Queen to Nana Mouskouri!" The very first song Mark bought for himself was the '80s number one 'Uptown Girl' by Billy Joel. He was also a Michael Jackson fan and even today says he would love to meet him. One of the first concerts Mark went to was Michael Jackson's HIStory in Dublin with Kian and Shane (who incidentally took a clump of grass home from the venue as a keepsake). Mark has always admired soulful Mariah Carey and therefore it was a great shock to find that she actually wanted to record with the boys. "At first we thought it was a joke... then we discovered she was serious and were knocked out," he says.

Bryan tells of how he used to sing Gary Barlow songs in karaoke and loved Take That, although he never went to see them play live because, "It was all girls!" He did, however, go and see Boyzone at their first gig in Dublin and also Backstreet Boys where he saw IO YOU as the support. Little did he know then that these guys were to become his fellow performers!

Westlife collectively proved their love of Motown when they appeared on the TV show Motown Mania. They performed versions of 'My Girl' and 'What Becomes Of The Brokenhearted'.

Coast to Coast

Westlife became record breakers when 'My Love' took the number one slot, making them the only band to have achieved seven consecutive number ones. "We're so proud to have done it... hopefully we'll have a few more," said Nicky. That was certainly no problem in 2001 on British shores. Westlife were honoured to be asked to record the single for Comic Relief. The song was a cover of Billy Joel's '80s hit 'Uptown Girl', coincidentally the first record Mark and Shane ever bought. It went straight to the top of the charts in March, making it Westlife's eighth consecutive number one. An amazing 292,318 copies were sold in the first week. "The band are proud to be a small part of such a worthwhile cause," said part of their team. In fact, proceeds from the single raised over £1 million for Comic Relief.

One of the greatest feats for British bands is to 'break America'. The first Westlife single released in the US was 'Swear It Again' and this was followed by a promotional tour. "America is the place where we want to build on our achievements," revealed Bryan. Westlife are determined they will be successful across the Atlantic and are now regularly getting airplay on radio stations 'coast to coast'!

PASSPORT

Mark

Full name:	Mark Michael Patrick Feehily
Date of birth:	28th May 1980
Star sign:	Gemini
Place of birth:	Sligo, Ireland
Height:	5ft 10in
Colour of eyes:	Blue
Parents:	Marie and Oliver
Siblings:	2 brothers - Barry, Colin
Pets:	Black labrador called Snoopy
Education:	St Patrick's National School, Summerhill College
Previous job(s):	Burger King, pizza delivery, photo shop assistant, the Feehily family conservatory business
First record bought:	Billy Joel's 'Uptown Girl'
Likes:	Alanis Morrissette, Mariah Carey, partying
Dislikes:	People who jump to conclusions too fast, smoking, fish
Sports:	Tennis, football
Favourite place in the world:	Sligo, Ireland

BRYAN:
UP CLOSE AND PERSONAL

"It was always my dream to appear on Top of the Pops."

Bryan is a real live-wire and, according to the Westlifers, is always on the go. He takes everything light-heartedly and enjoys playing jokes on the other guys in the band.

Young star

According to his family, Bryan has always been a cheeky chappie and was often into mischief as a young boy. He even tried running away from home! He didn't get very far though, only to the bus stop before he realised he didn't have any money!

As a child, Bryan loved to play football and explore in the country. He was a real daredevil, climbing trees and jumping from cliffs into the sea while on holiday.

Not surprisingly, Bryan's mum, Mairead, says it's been really quiet since Bryan left home! Since he was four, when he first joined the Billie Barry Stage School, Bryan was always singing around the house at the top of his voice. Billie Barry is famous for having helped the careers of many pop stars including Keavy and Edele from B*Witched and Mikey from Boyzone. Bryan rejoined the school when he was eight and won the first singing competition he entered. He learnt to tap dance and he and his sister Susan used to rehearse for hours at home. She joined Billie Barry and now treads the boards at home in Dublin in musicals. While at the school, Bryan appeared in lots of pantomimes, a production of The Wizard of Oz and later, the musical, Grease.

School life

When he went to secondary school, it was considered uncool to be at the Billie Barry and so Bryan was teased. He remembers hating school, but was bright and so stuck it out. Bryan admits he was a chubby kid when he was younger and because of it was picked on a lot. He reacted by becoming more and more cheeky. Bryan says he was never attractive to girls until he got to fifth or sixth year at school and only got his first kiss when he was 17!

When he left school, despite being told he could one day become a doctor, Bryan took an odd selection of jobs from bingo caller (which he says he loved) to supermarket assistant to working for security at McDonalds. The latter proved fairly rough and on one occasion Bryan feared for his life! Far safer was his role in a TV programme called Finbar's Class which he gained as a result of his time at Billie Barry. He played a character called Spot for about a year.

Making music

In 1997, Bryan formed a band called Cartel with two friends. They played all over Dublin and got quite a large fan base. Around this time, Bryan heard about the audition for what was to become Westlife. He learnt the news while in the hairdressers! The stylist spoke to his friend Louis Walsh about Bryan and so he was invited along to try out for the band.
The next stroke of luck Bryan had was seeing a neighbour as part of the TV crew filming the audition and so he managed to get to the front of the queue of wannabes.

Bryan remembers chatting to Nicky who he had met once or twice before around Dublin on karaoke nights. As one of the first to be seen at the audition, Bryan was disappointed to find he couldn't sing one of his own songs. He sang a Boyzone number instead... even though he didn't really know the words. "I sort of made them up as I went along," he laughs.

Bryan recalls his best moment with Westlife as hearing 'Swear It Again' on the radio for the first time. The most frustrating part of being in the band for Bryan is not getting to see family and friends as much as he'd like. He says his best mate is Eddie Loughlan who he has known since he was three. "We're soul mates, we do everything together," says Bryan.

With the success he's achieved, Bryan hopes to secure a good future for his sister and family. He says fame certainly hasn't gone to his head and it's nothing like he expected. From the very outset, the boys promised themselves they wouldn't change and Bryan believes they've stuck to it.

GREEN GREEN GRASS OF HOME

They say 'home is where the heart is' and for Westlife this certainly rings true. Ask any of the boys where they would most like to take time out and the answer is always the same – back at home with family and friends.

Homework

The boys recorded the video for 'My Love' in Ireland and for this reason it's particularly special to them. The venue was actually County Clare on the far west coast of Ireland, just a few hours from the boys' home towns of Sligo and Dublin. It meant a welcome change from flying into international airports and getting jet lag for the video recording – even though it was a little cooler than some locations!

It was at Westlife's request that the video was shot on home ground. Shane explained how there could be no other place to sing the lines 'Overseas, coast to coast, back to the place that we love the most'. Mark adds, "It's brilliant to be able to show off to the world where we come from. We probably would appeal to kids more than any tourist magazine."

R & R (rest and relaxation)

Given their busy schedule, returning home is a real treat for Westlife. When they get there, the boys are more likely to enjoy a quiet night in than going out clubbing. "When you're in this sort of business, you appreciate the simple things like just sitting on your own sofa with a cup of tea chatting with family and friends," says Mark.

Kian reckons there's nothing quite like waking up at home and seeing familiar things. Pride of place on Kian's bedroom wall are the Westlife gold discs. Family comes first with Kian and every trip home means catching up with the Egan clan. He is uncle to Rea and Gavin, his sister's children and loves to play with them.

Being recognised is one of the penalties of being a world famous pop star. Kian is used to fans coming round to his parents' house and says his family have learned to adjust their lives since Westlife's success. He says thankfully most people in Sligo treat him normally when he goes home. Like each of the Westlife boys, Kian doesn't expect any special treatment and prefers to be able to relax during his precious time off.

Since the band's rapid rise to fame, family and friends are protective of Kian. He says his mum does worry about him because of Westlife's hectic schedule. Kian's mates look out for their famous friend. "When we're on a night out, they won't let me walk home since Westlife became so famous, they make me call a cab," he laughs.

Bryan finds the pressures of fame hard and misses being part of the gang back home in Dublin. He says his friends do now treat him a bit differently which can be upsetting, but he has grown used to it. Bryan says he misses the down to earth pubs of Dublin and would much rather be at home with his mates than in the glitzy bars of London. "They really don't have the same atmosphere. In a Dublin pub there's always singing and laughter," he says.

Being homesick is something the boys are coming to terms with. In the early days, of Westlife, Mark said that being away for even two weeks at a time meant they would be dying to get back. "Now we're so used to each other's company, we can go away for a lot longer without feeling too bad... but we still do miss home."

SHANE:
UP CLOSE AND PERSONAL

"I always wanted to be in a band."

Young Shane Filan grew up in the centre of Sligo, West Ireland. He was singing just as soon as he could talk. Shane's mum, Mae, was not surprised by her son's achievements. "He was always singing and entertaining. I never doubted Shane would succeed, he was always very determined," she says.

Shane made his first public performance as a toddler singing a few lines during an election campaign in his home town of Sligo. Mae still keeps the first microphone he made for himself when he was four. "I was a really big pop fan," says Shane. He remembers first singing Billy Joel songs and then Michael Jackson songs. Shane says he took much inspiration from Michael Jackson who, to this day, remains his musical hero.

Mum's the word

Shane also has great admiration for his mum and dad. "They've been really supportive and I'm so proud of them," he says. Shane says his mum has been a driving force in his life as she has been with all her children. In fact, it was Mae who made the all-important call to manager, Louis Walsh, in the early days. Dad, Peter, who also has a great voice, helped with young Shane's singing technique.

Shane was the youngest in the Filan household. He has six brothers and sisters and admits he was a bit spoilt. The Filan family are very close and Shane is proud to be godfather to his brother Finbarr's first child, Killian. Shane enjoys watching his godson singing in front of the TV with his microphone, much the same as he did himself. The Filans are a religious family and Shane tells how his mum has a holy medal which she blesses each time he goes home. Shane says his prayers every night before he goes to sleep and goes to church every Sunday where possible.

As a child, Shane took to the stage whenever he could. He joined local theatre companies as well as performing in school plays. Grease is particularly familiar to Shane – he has appeared in it no less than four times, twice playing Danny. It was during rehearsals for one production at secondary school he first got to know Kian. Shane says he really enjoyed acting and wouldn't mind treading the boards again in the future.

Sporting student

Shane was a pretty good student at school and, on odd occasions when he did mess around, he made sure he never got caught! After school and in the holidays, Shane would help out at his mum and dad's restaurant in Sligo. It's one they have run for many years, even before Shane was on the scene. If he wasn't helping with the family business, you could usually find Shane out playing football or rugby. He also excelled at kick-boxing. Following in his brothers' footsteps, Shane took his rugby seriously and, at 15, he stopped singing for about a year to concentrate on playing for the Connacht team.

The Filans own a number of horses and Shane has always loved spending time looking after them. When he goes home now, he visits the stables and usually takes out one of his favourites. Shane has entered many showjumping contests with his brothers and the Filan house is full of trophies from their successes. Shane still likes to visit The Horse of the Year Show, a prestigious date in the horseman's calendar.

Making it big

Shane left college, where he was studying accountancy, to join the original band. He recalls the early days: "We knew we were going to have to work really hard in the first few years to make Westlife a success." Often hailed as the front man of the band, Shane sees Westlife more as a team effort and is very modest about his talents. He says he's just doing what he loves - singing.

Shane's best friend in Westlife is Nicky. They first met back in 1997, when Nicky auditioned for the band. They hit it off immediately, even though Shane thought Nicky a little quiet. Today, they always share a room when touring and enjoy many 'not so quiet' nights out on the town. According to Shane, they think alike, enjoy doing the same things, like the same clothes and even the same girls! Shane has said he wishes he had the kind of partner Nicky has in Georgina. Consequently, Nicky has tried matchmaking! However Shane reckons he wouldn't be very reliable as a boyfriend now, given the amount of time Westlife spend out of the country.

Shane is passionate about his work and takes it very seriously. In Westlife, he says he is living out a dream as he has always wanted to be on stage entertaining. He accepts being in the band has made him mature very quickly, but says it hasn't really changed him as a person.

COMPETITION

Get your hands on some of the hottest Westlife merchandise around. We are offering 2 packs of Westlife goodies to the lucky winners of our competition and 20 posters for the runners up.

All you have to do is answer the simple question below and explain, in no more than 20 words, the reason why you are the No.1 Westlife fan.

Which song did Westlife record for Comic Relief in 2001?

Write your answers on a postcard or the back of a sealed envelope (don't forget to put your name, address and age) and post to the following address:
Westlife Competition, Egmont Books Limited, Unit 7, Millbank House, Riverside Park, Bollin Walk, Wilmslow, Cheshire SK9 1BJ.
To arrive no later than January 25th, 2002

Rules
1) 2 winners will be chosen at random and notified by post.
2) Judges' decision is final. No correspondence will be entered into.
3) The winners' names will be made available from Egmont Books Ltd, (on request) after February 8th, 2002. Please enclose a stamped addressed envelope for reply.
4) Employees (and their relatives) of Egmont Books Limited and their associated companies are not eligible to enter.
5) Entries are limited to one per person.
6) Competition is open to residents of the UK, Channel Islands, and Ireland only.
7) The Publishers reserve the right to vary prizes, subject to availability.
8) Closing date for entries is January 25th, 2002.

 # ON THE ROAD

From Birmingham to Brisbane, Westlife have certainly made their mark. They first played Wembley Arena as the support for Boyzone, and now they are the topping the bill!

The buzz

The boys' enthusiasm for live performance was evident from the outset. As part of IO YOU with Kian and Shane, Mark recalls one of his earliest concerts as the support for Backstreet Boys: "I can't describe the level of excitement. We used to get a buzz out of playing for 200 people in a nightclub, now this was multiplied by infinity!"

Ever since the early concerts with IO YOU, the boys have performed a ritual just before going on stage. They form a circle, lock hands in the centre, count to three in Irish and shout the band's name.

Looking after the boys on the road is tour manager Anto Byrne. He ensures everything runs smoothly. He also keeps the boys on their toes as he is the practical joker of the team. He has ample opportunity for fun on long plane journeys and on one occasion particularly enjoyed winding up Kian by taking the new Rolex from his wrist while he slept. The boys enjoy playing tricks on each other too, often by painting the face of an unsuspecting snoozer!

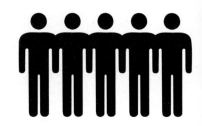

Despite the fact that Bryan sees it as the time for chatting up air hostesses, long plane journeys give the boys chance to catch up on some rest. On one trip to Australia however, the plane journey proved no time for sleep – the flight was hit by bad turbulence and the plane was struck by lightning, not just once, but four times!

Having such a busy schedule, the boys have adjusted to grabbing sleep as and when the opportunity arises. Mark is particularly adept. "I once fell asleep in a helicopter," he says. "We were in South East Asia swooping down over all this amazing landscape and next thing I knew we were landing at the hotel!"

The US and beyond

Touring with Westlife might be a lot of fun, but it isn't all plain sailing. In the summer of 2000, the boys began a promotional tour of America which was beset with difficulties. As well as an exhausting non-stop schedule, the travel arrangements were fraught with disasters. On arrival in Denver after a 24-hour flight, the boys found they had nowhere to stay. They then found their luggage was on its way to Omaha! Only a few days later, after a whirlwind recording session with Mariah Carey in Italy, the boys were back in trouble when they landed in North Carolina shortly after a tornado had wiped out all the electricity, thus cancelling their show.

Towards the end of the tour, the schedule proved too much for the boys. They were stressed and emotional. Mark recalls, "It really started to get to us. We'd been doing exactly the same thing for two months and completed everything that was asked of us. But eventually we took a stand." Concerned for their health and emotional well-being, the boys had a serious chat about the touring schedule. Postponing part of their Latin American tour, they returned home to Dublin to talk to their manager, Louis.

The promotional trip which followed took in Japan, Korea and Singapore. Here, Westlife landed to thousands of excited fans at Changi airport. In this part of the world, Coast to Coast achieved double platinum status in just a few weeks. Media from all over South East Asia, India, Australia and New Zealand gathered for a press conference. Journalists and photographers enjoyed a friendly football match where Westlife were up against competition winners and local celebs. The four week tour did, however, prove tough, and the boys speak of it as the time they have been most homesick.

Going global

Westlife began their most extensive tour to date in the UK on 9th February 2001. It kicked off in Newcastle and encompassed 54 dates, totalling an audience of 500,000 fans. Tickets for the dates sold in minutes. The boys commented, "Our UK tour is what we've been working towards over the last few years. We can't imagine anything more thrilling than performing live in Britain and seeing the excitement on our fans' faces."

Nicky got himself into shape and increased his stamina for the shows by returning to his football training regime. Mark explained how excited the band were and how they had all contributed ideas to the live show. "We want everyone to go home thinking it was a great show," he said. There was no doubt of that. The shows went down a storm and included special remixes of Westlife's hits.

The UK tour concluded in Birmingham on 19th April. The boys then took to the road in Ireland, across to Europe, South East Asia, Australia, New Zealand and South America.

It was the boys' second visit to South America. This time they knew what to expect having been closely chaperoned and given a bodyguard each on their first visit. In Argentina, the riot police had even showed up in case any of the boys were kidnapped!

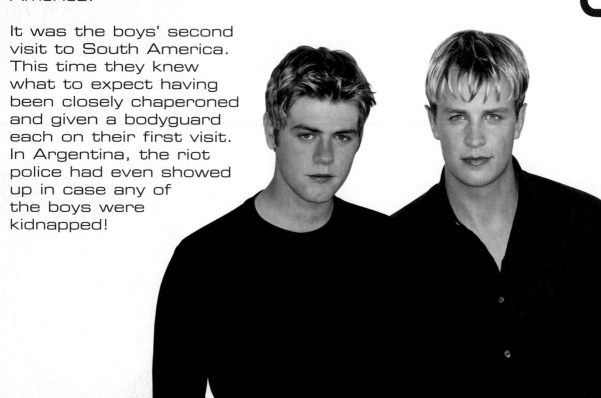

No place like home

Video shoots also see Westlife travelling to exotic locations around the globe. When they went to Acapulco for a shoot, Mark was so impressed he went back there for a holiday. All the boys travelled to Mexico City for the video of 'Fool Again' where hundreds of locals gazed in wonder as they performed on the roof of a forty-storey building.

Shane says of all the places he's visited with Westlife his favourite is Sydney, Australia. Nicky also loved Oz, but says it's definitely too far from home.

For Westlife, the best place in the world is always going to be Ireland. "There's nothing like the feeling of going home," says Shane.

Full name:	Kian John Francis Egan
Date of birth:	29th April 1980
Star sign:	Taurus
Place of birth:	Sligo, Ireland
Height:	5ft 8½in
Colour of eyes:	Blue
Distinguishing feature(s):	Scar under right eye, tattoo on right ankle
Parents:	Patricia and Kevin
Siblings:	3 brothers - Gavin, Tom, Colm 3 sisters - Vivienne, Fenelle, Marielle
Education:	Scoil Ursula, St John's, Summerhill College
Previous job(s):	Clothes shop assistant, kissagram
First record bought:	Metallica
Likes:	A good night out, performing, playing piano
Dislikes:	Rude people, sushi
Worst habit:	Biting nails
Sports:	Football, basketball, golf
Car:	Black BMW
Favourite place in the world:	Home

Loved up

They are one of the most talked about bands in pop. Speculation runs high on Westlife romances and it seems everyone wants to know the intimate details of the boys' personal lives. So let's take a look at some Westlife secrets and how the boys really rate in the romance stakes!

Baby love

When the boys were younger the challenge was to see who could snog the most girls in a night. Kian reckons he was the winner as he once clocked up 12!

For Kian, it was never too early to start romancing the girls. He says he had his first girlfriend when he was just five! The young lady in question lived over the road from the Egans. However once he started school, his mum reports he was really shy and wouldn't even sit next to a girl.

These days, Kian is a romantic and says the ultimate for him would be to take a girl away to a log cabin in the mountains for Christmas. His favourite British celeb ladies are Martine McCutcheon and Cat Deeley. On US shores, Kian would love to meet Sarah Michelle Gellar from Buffy, Jennifer Lopez and Jennifer Aniston.

Public romance

Bryan says he likes to get to know someone before going out on a date. His ideal lady is one who makes him laugh and makes him happy. He may have found his dream girl in Kerry of Atomic Kitten. The relationship was made public by the press while the couple were on holiday and Bryan says although he was angry at the invasion of their privacy, in a way it was a relief to no longer hide his feelings.

Bryan says he's madly in love. When the boys played at London's Astoria, he spent most of the evening performing directly at Kerry. She showed her support by wearing a 'Westlife for Christmas Number One' t-shirt in the audience. After their first Christmas together, Bryan said it had been his best ever.

Bryan admits it is particularly difficult to have a relationship when both parties are in the public eye because everyone's always waiting for something to go wrong. He has said maybe it would have been easier to fall for someone who's not well-known.

Nicky is also in a serious relationship and is devoted to Georgina, his girlfriend of over five years. Georgina is the daughter of Irish Prime Minister Bertie Ahern.

For Nicky, the way to attract a girl is by eye contact. Not so for Shane, he just bowls straight over and says hello if he fancies a girl. Shane's ideal romantic night is being with a loved one in front of the fire – woolly socks and all! In response to the question 'What makes a man?' Shane admits he hasn't got a clue. Maybe charm, humour and Irish eyes! When it comes to females in the public eye, Shane has a soft spot for Faith Hill, Donna Air, Cat Deeley and he says Faye from Steps is also quite fanciable.

Mark admits he's no Casanova: "I've not got much confidence when it comes to girls... I'm quite bad at chatting them up." For Mark, the band is much more important than any girl at the moment.

From the very outset, it was established that Westlife comes first. The boys have made personal sacrifices to keep Westlife at the top, but no doubt would all agree, it's been worth it.

MARK:
UP CLOSE AND PERSONAL

"I'm grateful I've been given a talent."

He's described as very laid back, always up for a laugh and certainly not as quiet as he seems. His favourite phrase is 'It will sort itself out'. Yes, Mark Feehily is the Westlifer who takes everything in his stride.

Stage presence

Being up on stage with Westlife is when Mark feels most confident. With the other guys in the band he's not at all quiet, but he can be shy with those he doesn't know or if he's unexpectedly put in the spotlight. Mark likes his privacy and often enjoys quality time on his own.

He's certainly not as image conscious as some of the Westlifers and admits he doesn't really think about his appearance. Mark believes money is of little importance, as long as you're comfortable.

The most important thing for Mark is singing. He isn't bothered by fame and says he'd be just as happy without it as long as he was with the band. One of his best moments with Westlife has to be recording with Mariah Carey. Mark is crazy about the singer and was overawed when she agreed to work with the boys. Mark has said in the future he'd like to write a song especially for her.

Nursery start

Mark's dad, Oliver, says Mark got his first taste of music when he was still in his cot. Putting the radio beside him was the only way to get baby Mark off to sleep! One of Mark's earliest performances was uncannily singing 'Uptown Girl'. The occasion was his playschool end of term concert! So, while the other kids sang nursery rhymes, Mark was preparing for a future in pop!

From that time on, Mark was always singing. Even today, the other guys say he sings all day long. Mark liked to play tennis and badminton when he was younger, but nothing compared to performing. He took part in plenty of talent contests. One was particularly memorable – he completely forgot the words to the song! As well as singing with the school choir and the choir at his parish church, Mark joined the National Children's Choir. He also learnt to play the tin whistle and remembers making up his own tunes.

Mark admits that after being really shy on joining his first school, he was then really noisy and messy and probably his teacher's worst nightmare! His favourite school subject was French, after going on an exchange which he loved. Mark took part in his first musical at primary school. It was called Scrooged, a show based on the story of Scrooge.

Country boy

Mark grew up about two miles outside of Sligo. He says he didn't visit the town much until he went to secondary school. Instead he used to just hang out with his cousins who lived close by.

Mark goes home as often as possible. He likes to chill out and take a walk in the country with his kid brothers, Colin and Barry. Mark says Barry is really shy right now, just like he was at his age. The Feehily family have four horses – Star, Freddy, Charlie and Jenny – and Mark loves to spend time with them.

When he's away, Mark phones home at least once a day and is very protective of his family who have supported him throughout his career. For Mark, Mum is the most important person in the world and he values her opinions on everything... even girls! He says, "If I was serious about someone, it would be important my mum liked them because I love her more than anything." However, Mark doesn't agree with searching desperately for the right girl: "I believe if it's meant to happen, it will some day."

Looking to the future, Mark says he'd like to build his own home close to Sligo, but it would have to be near a lake or the sea as he quite fancies getting himself a jet ski! As far as Westlife are concerned, Mark wants them to be the best band in the world. He believes if a song is great, it will always shine through. After Westlife? Mark says he will always be in the entertainment business, whether it's recording or writing his own songs.

PASSPORT

Bryan

Full name:	Bryan Nicholas McFadden
Date of birth:	12th April 1980
Star sign:	Aries
Place of birth:	Dublin, Ireland
Height:	6ft 2in
Colour of eyes:	Blue
Distinguishing feature(s):	Birthmark on lower back
Parents:	Mairead and Brendan
Siblings:	1 sister - Susan
Pets:	A Shih Tzu, Chip
Education:	St Fiachra's, St David's CBS Primary, St David's Secondary, St Joseph's Rosmini
Previous job(s):	Bingo caller, McDonalds' security
First record bought:	Kylie Minogue's 'I Should Be So Lucky'
Likes:	Spending money, girls
Dislikes:	Violence, rats
Worst habit:	Being forgetful
Sports:	Football, golf
Car:	Black Mercedes

PASSPORT APPR

Westlife fans are spread far and wide and each and every one is important to the boys. They say they really appreciate all the support their fans give them and enjoy meeting them whenever possible.

The Westlife boys are accustomed to being mobbed by fans wherever they go. However, having hundreds of screaming girls running behind you can sometimes be a little scary. Shane remembers one time when a fan actually pulled down his trousers and he was left baring his pants to all in Dublin town centre!

While on tour, the boys love playing to a live audience and are constantly amused by the fans' banners which often reveal some cheeky messages. Nicky says some of the fans are unbelievable: "They stand just inches from you and scream their heads off!" Kian recalls the most frantic of record shop signings in Edinburgh. Apparently 6000 fans showed up, and almost half met the band and went home with autographs.

Both Kian and Shane admit they have dated fans and you'll be pleased to know the others say they would consider doing so too, if they were single!

Westlife out East

Westlife have fans around the world, but undoubtedly the craziest are those from South East Asia. Kian remembers the fans on their first visit to Malaysia: "They not only grab you to touch you, they actually try to get a piece of you!"

Nicky says they're equally as frantic in Indonesia. On arrival there, the boys were besieged outside the airport and barely made the transition to their bus as girls grabbed their hair, personal possessions and clothes. Nicky remembers the mayhem: "Once we'd all got on the bus, the fans started rocking it!" Fans here were so persistent, the boys had two security guards each throughout their stay. One day, the boys returned to their hotel rooms to find fans had somehow managed to get in. The following scene was reportedly manic with security yelling at everyone and girls crying. Nicky explains how difficult it is to calm the fans when they don't speak your language: "In some cases, it's just a matter of run for your life!"

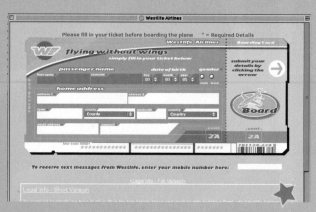

Keeping in touch

Westlife like to thank fans for their support whenever possible. They made a special 'Coast to Coast' day to travel the length of the UK to express their gratitude. The journey took in Glasgow, where the boys made a store appearance, press conference and photo call, Manchester for more of the same, Birmingham and finally London. "We'd liked to have spent more time with people and made it more personal if we could," said Bryan at the end of an exhausting day.

To find out more about Westlife, why not join the fan club? Write to: The Official Westlife Fanclub, PO Box 50, Stanmore, Middlesex, HA7 2US. On joining, you will receive the magazine This is…Westlife (and subsequent editions), five photo biography cards, membership card and occasional surprise gifts.

Westlife are also on the net. Their impressive official site can be reached at **www.westlife.co.uk**. When you enter, you will be greeted by 'This is your Captain speaking, please choose your country of departure…'. To board and explore Westlife Airlines you initially need to register your details, and you can even receive text messages from the band by entering your mobile phone number. Once you have completed your boarding card, you can explore the plane. In the lounge, you are invited to 'Sit back, relax and enjoy the inflight entertainment…'. You will find seated each of the boys with biographies, photo albums and personal messages. You can venture into the cockpit for the Westlife chat room, message board, latest news, events and tour dates.

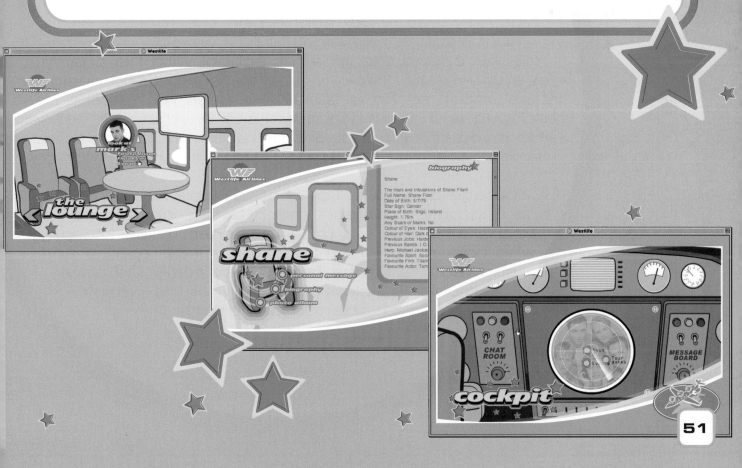

NICKY:
UP CLOSE AND PERSONAL

"I always loved singing. Any excuse to get on stage and sing, I was there."

One of Nicky's earliest dreams was to play at Wembley. He's certainly fulfilled that ambition, even though his first thoughts might have been aimed at the footie pitch!

Football crazy

Nicky Byrne is known for his footballing skills as well as his performing skills. Ever since the age of two, Nicky has been kicking the football around with his dad at the family home in Baldoyle, North Dublin.

Not only was Nicky scoring on the football pitch, mum Yvonne remembers him winning over the teachers (and the girls) at school with his charm. As a youngster, Nicky was into fashion and designer labels, much as he is today. He says he had the best childhood and never went without anything he needed. He loved to sing in front of family and friends and remembers getting on stage at his aunt's wedding.

By the age of about 15, football was proving Nicky's one and only interest – much to the distress of his teachers! It was his music teacher, Miss Murphy, who convinced Nicky to sit his music exams and showed the Byrne family they really did have a musically talented son (when he wasn't on the football pitch)!

Nicky spent two years as an apprentice at Leeds United and combined this with some modelling work. He used to play in goal and, while training, met with one of his childhood heroes, Lee Sharpe. It was only a short space of time before he was to meet with another of his heroes, Ronan Keating.

Karaoke king

On his return to Ireland, Nicky invested in a karaoke machine and worked with his dad staging karaoke nights around Dublin. "I was used to seeing my dad up on stage as he's in a cabaret band. I asked him to help me out because he was better on stage. We had a real good laugh," remembers Nicky. Working these nights, Nicky gained valuable experience and confidence at performing. At the start of each session, Nicky would sing a few songs, then his dad would take to the stage and then the last song of the night would be Nicky's.

Nicky found his way into Westlife after his girlfriend's aunt drew his attention to an advertisement for the Dublin audition. Nicky promptly set up the well-used karaoke machine in his lounge and spent all day practising the songs 'Isn't It A Wonder' (by Boyzone) and the Irish songs 'The Town I Loved So Well' and 'She Moved Through The Fair'. He made recordings of the numbers and sent them to Louis Walsh with his photograph. When Nicky received the call for the audition, he set off for Dublin in his best suit. "I went with everything crossed and sang my heart out," he remembers.

With just 30 others (out of approximately 300 hopefuls), Nicky was excited to get the call back for a second audition the following weekend. After watching Bryan perform, Nicky went on stage and sang the Boyzone track 'Words'. "I don't think I sang it all that well," he says, "but next thing we knew, it was down to just Bryan and me." Their ordeal was not over yet. There was a dance routine to perform and Nicky was nervous. "It wasn't me at all," he says. Despite his footballing feet, Nicky managed to impress Louis and the other boys and the band were on their way.

Home sweet home

There's no place like home for Nicky. According to his mum, Nicky is a born worrier and more often than not rings home every day. He has said he wishes he could time travel to fit in all the promotions, photo shoots, and other commitments without missing out on quality time at home.

When he is back home, Nicky loves to catch up with family and friends, maybe going fishing with his dad or playing a round or two of golf. Nicky reckons the sport is pretty addictive and it seems all the Westlifers have taken to the golf course. "We're very competitive and always play for money!" says Nicky. "All my friends back home are into golf too, so whenever I go home, it's all I want to do."

Despite missing family and friends, Nicky says working with Westlife is everything he's ever wanted. He acknowledges the fact that Westlife can't always have number ones. "We'll just keep working as hard as we can," he says. He is best buddies with Shane and says they often confide in each other which is really reassuring when they are away from home. They also like to party and have named their notorious nights out together 'Shnicky' nights.

Looking to the future, Nicky has plenty of aspirations. He says he would like to do a solo track, maybe some presenting and play football again in front of a big crowd. Nicky would like to see soccer as popular in Ireland as it is in England. He is keen to get involved with the League of Ireland and build a new stadium in the North of Dublin – of course, near to his home!

The Westlife™ Challenge

How much do you really know about Westlife? Take the Westlife Challenge and find out just how keen a fan you really are.
Answers can be found on the opposite page... but no cheating!

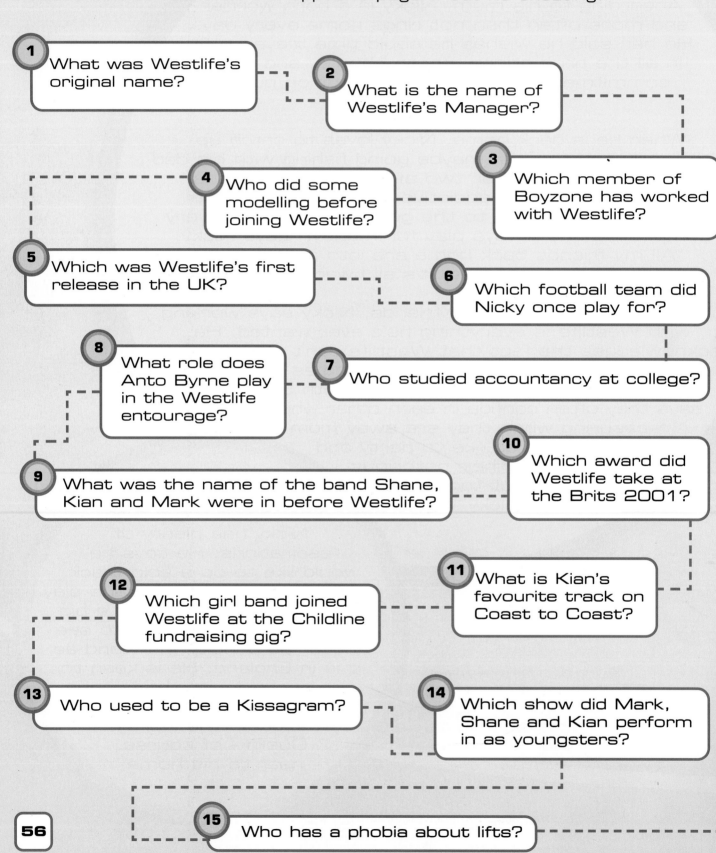

1 What was Westlife's original name?

2 What is the name of Westlife's Manager?

3 Which member of Boyzone has worked with Westlife?

4 Who did some modelling before joining Westlife?

5 Which was Westlife's first release in the UK?

6 Which football team did Nicky once play for?

7 Who studied accountancy at college?

8 What role does Anto Byrne play in the Westlife entourage?

9 What was the name of the band Shane, Kian and Mark were in before Westlife?

10 Which award did Westlife take at the Brits 2001?

11 What is Kian's favourite track on Coast to Coast?

12 Which girl band joined Westlife at the Childline fundraising gig?

13 Who used to be a Kissagram?

14 Which show did Mark, Shane and Kian perform in as youngsters?

15 Who has a phobia about lifts?

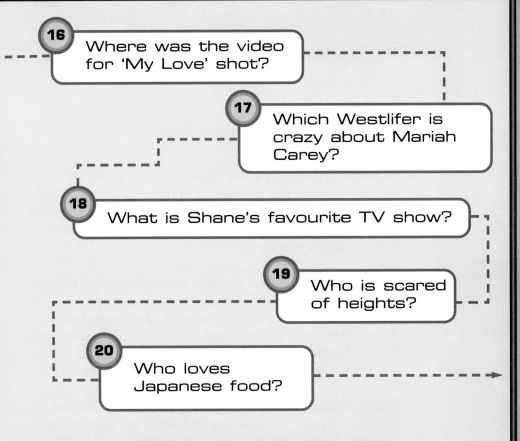

16 Where was the video for 'My Love' shot?

17 Which Westlifer is crazy about Mariah Carey?

18 What is Shane's favourite TV show?

19 Who is scared of heights?

20 Who loves Japanese food?

How well did you do?

20 correct answers: Westlife Superfan – Congratulations! You really know your stuff. Go to the top of the class. Are you sure you didn't sneak a look at the answers?

15-20 correct answers: 1st class fan – Well done! There certainly were some tricky ones thrown in for fun! Make sure you keep up with all the latest news and you'll become a Superfan in no time!

10-15 correct answers: Fan – Well, you did okay, but there's lots of room for improvement.

Under 10 correct answers: You are the weakest link! Do you really know who Westlife are? You'd better get down to some serious reading and try a lot harder next time!

20. Nicky.

19. Bryan.

18. Friends.

17. Mark.

16. Co. Clare, Ireland.

15. Nicky.

14. Grease.

13. Kian.

12. Atomic Kitten.

11. 'What makes a man'

10. Best Pop Act.

9. 10 YOU.

8. Tour Manager.

7. Shane.

6. Leeds United.

5. Swear It Again.

4. Nicky.

3. Ronan Keating.

2. Louis Walsh.

1. Westside.

Westlife have certainly taken the world of pop music by storm. They have thousands of fans worldwide and have been compared to The Beatles with their string of number one hits.

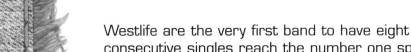

Record breakers

Westlife are the very first band to have eight consecutive singles reach the number one spot. And all this was in less than two years. They have achieved number one albums and sales in excess of seven million copies worldwide.

Nicky puts their success down to the fact that there's no boss in the band. "We all have our own opinions and we're our own bosses," he says. In the crucial early days, Westlife was privileged to have sound advice from Ronan Keating who, from first hand experience, knew the boys' concerns and the pressures they were under.

Shane says he and the boys are proud of what they have achieved: "We just try and work as hard as we can and enjoy what we do." Shane saw performing at the Royal Albert Hall for the People's Choice Awards as an important moment in their careers. "The mature audience was from the industry and they all stopped what they were doing and were glued to us," he recalls proudly.

Award winners

Westlife have received accolades, in the form of awards, right around the globe. Their awards have included Indonesia's Voice of the 21st Century for Shane, in South Africa, Best Love Song 1999 for 'Swear It Again' and in Norway, Topp magazine's award for Best Band of the Year 1999.

In the UK, awards have flooded in from the outset. Westlife won Smash Hits Best New Tour Act 1998, Record of the Year 1999 for Flying Without Wings and TV Hits Best New Act 1999. In 2000, for the second year running, Westlife were winners of Brittania's Record of the Year for 'My Love'. They were also voted MTV Europe's Best Pop Act. At the Brits 2001, they were nominated in three categories and walked away with the title of Best Pop Act. They dedicated the award to their fans.

The price of fame

Westlife have proved themselves adept at answering difficult questions at press conferences all over the world. Mark, however, has said there are times when the line must be drawn in order to retain some privacy: "We'd surely go insane if everything about us was public. Sometimes the questions have no relevance at all to our music and so it shouldn't make a difference."

The boys have become accustomed to a life in the public eye. It is media pressure, as well as being away from family and friends so much, which is the down side of being so successful. Mark says the thing he's discovered through fame is that money isn't really important, it's family and friends which matter. For Shane, one of the worst parts of fame is meeting people who pretend to be one of their best friends when they hardly know them.

Often the boys return home for a taste of normality. Although fans do know their private addresses, being back at home with all the family keeps the boys' feet firmly on the ground.

The boys say coping with success is sometimes hard, but there's no escaping the fact they have a dream job and wouldn't change it for anything.

Flying high

Westlife are full of ambition. Their short term aim is to secure success in America. The long term plan is to make at least five albums and match that with tours, although of course it does all depend on the continued support of you, the fans.

DISC O GRAPHY

TOP TEN
19TH APRIL 1999

		Swear It Again
1	Westlife	
2		
3		
4		
5		
6		

TOP TEN SINGLES
9TH AUGUST 1999

		If I Let You Go
1	Westlife	
2		
3		

A NEWSPAPER 18th October 1999

TOP OF THE POPS
TOP SINGLES

1. (-) **Flying Without Wings**
   – Westlife

2.

ALBUM CHARTS
1st November 1999

1		
2	Westlife	Over 1 million copies sold
3		

TOP TEN-SINGLES
13th December 1999

		I Have A Dream/Seasons In The Sun
1	Westlife	
2		
3		
4		
5		
6		

4 Times Platinum!

SINGLES CHART
27th March 2000

1	Westlife	Fool Again
2		
3		
4		

CHART POSITIONS
18TH SEPTEMBER 2000

1	Against All Odds	Westlife with Mariah Carey
2		

TOP OF THE POPS
30th October 2000

1	Westlife	My Love

NEWSPAPER 6th November 2000

HOT CHARTS
TOP ALBUMS

1. (-) **Coast To Coast**
   – Westlife

4.

Double Platinum!

THE NEWSPAPER 5th March 2001

HOT CHARTS
TOP TEN SINGLES

1. (-) **Uptown Girl**
   – Westlife

2.

HIT PARADE
2nd July 2001

	Westlife	When You're Looking Like That

61